GW00390868

YORK AS IT WAS

by

Ronald Willis

Cover picture: Blossom Street and Micklegate Bar c. 1850 from a lithograph by Monkhouse. (By courtesy of Yorkshire Architectural and York Archaeological Society.)

First Edition – March 1973
Second Impression – February 1975
Third Impression – February 1977
Fourth Impression – May 1981
Fifth Impression – April 1984

Published by Hendon Publishing Co. Ltd., Hendon Mill, Nelson.
Printed by: Fretwell & Brian Ltd., Healey Works, Goulbourne St., Keighley, West Yorkshire BD21 1PZ.

ACKNOWLEDGEMENTS

The author wishes to thank Mr. O. S. Tomlinson, F.L.A., York City Librarian; Mr. Maurice Smith, A.L.A., York City Reference Librarian; the Yorkshire Architectural and York Archaeological Society; the Yorkshire Evening Press; British Rail; and the Royal Commission on Historical Monuments (England), for the photographs used in this publication.

THE AUTHOR

Ronald Willis is Deputy Features Editor of The Yorkshire Evening Press, York. His other works include Portrait Of York, published in 1972 by Robert Hale, The Living Past and Nonconformist Chapels of York 1693-1840.

YORK AS IT WAS

FACED with photographs from another century, we are all time travellers, seeing the streets of our cities sleepy and shuttered in the ancient warmth, catching the fugitive scent of the past. As the sunlight fell on house and corner shop, on church and quiet square, it helped the camera pin down a moment in time, like a fly in amber. The workaday scenes are at once familiar and strange. Streets are narrower, buildings lower, advertising less controlled, colours darker, clothes drabber.

But in the historic cities the great monuments are untouched by a mere century. The rich texture of gothic stonework, fissured by sun and frost, takes the ages in its stride. In York, the triple-towered Minster and attendant churches have formed an unchanging backdrop to the developing social life on stage, as it exchanged carriages and crinolines for cars and mini-skirts.

For most of us, it is the day before yesterday which holds the greatest interest; pictures of the city on the very boundary of living memory. The humble shops, long replaced by the facades of the multiple stores, are seen to possess a rare individuality, whether they are selling paper-wrapped stovepipe hats or tobaccos with strange names. The richness lies in the details, rarely in the decorative aspect of the buildings, for there seems to have been a lack of imagination in our ancestors' painting schemes. When the eighteenth-century Black Swan, the famous Coney Street coaching inn (four days to London, God willing) was demolished in the 1950's, it was found, on examination of the paint layers on its door pillars that, with a very brief exception, they had been slightly varying shades of buff for two centuries.

From a vantage point high on the medieval city wall as it strode over the tracks, an early photographer has caught the dark vaporous air of the city's first railway station, familiar to Charles Dickens on his many visits, not only to give his famous readings, but to visit his brother and sister-in-law. Looking like a Gustave Dore engraving, the ghostly trainshed of 1841 (demolished in December 1966) was built at a time when mail-coaches still rattled north from London, and when the ringing shot from a flintlock pistol warned platelayers of approaching trains. This intramural depot, superseded a century ago by the dynamically curved mainline station outside the city wall, was the tourists' introduction to early and mid-Victorian York as they arrived bolt upright in the cramped carriages, equipped in winter with foot-warmers.

Remarkably advanced for its time (the iron and glass construction caused considerable delays) the station replaced a two-roomed wooden hut with a staff of two, the company secretary and the booking clerk, who sold tickets in 1839 for the first railway journey from York—a trial trip to Copmanthorpe and back which took the then reasonable time of 40 minutes. First class on that pioneer journey was for directors of the line; second class for "respectable persons". The engine, named Lowther, had been built by the Stephensons of Newcastle, and carried all the latest improvements. The carriage for the 18 directors and their friends was, according to a contemporary report, "fitted up in a style of elegance far exceeding anything we have ever before observed in any public carriage." During the trip a speed of 15 to 20 mph was reached and "horses grazing in adjoining fields capered about at a most fearful rate."

A month later York was connected to the Leeds and Selby line at Milford Junction, and for the official opening of the York and North Midland Railway the city was festive with bells, flags and booming cannon. The company advertised its intentions in the local newspaper under a block of a prettily-drawn, tall-stacked locomotive hauling the different classes of coach. This time there was a third-class carriage for the brass band. Reports said the travellers were borne along with the speed of a racehorse, though the return journey was slower to allow passengers to see different parts of the line and—curious phrase—"to view the moving landscape". The Guildhall, brilliantly lit by gas as dusk dropped, was the scene of a celebration dinner with George Stephenson sitting on the Lord Mayor's right. The champagne flowed "till the cloth was drawn" and a grand ball at the Mansion House lasted until dawn. These were the beginnings of our own railway nostalgia.

The city bestrides the oldest highway of all—the River Ouse—running its looping course to the Humber and the North Sea. At its junction with the tiny River Foss it creates a thin tongue of land, St. George's Field. It was not here, but further upstream that the Roman Ninth Legion camped on its arrival from Lincoln in AD71. In time, the Roman fortress and civil town occupied opposite sides of the river, the military centre, its impressive limestone walls shot through with a decorative red tile band, holding the east bank. The town houses and baths of the Colonia spread over what is now Bishophill.

Five bridges now span the main stream. The oldest is Ouse Bridge of 1810; the youngest, Clifton Bridge, opened in 1963. The Scarborough rail and footbridge took the line coastwards in 1844, while the Lendal and Skeldergate Bridges date from the second half of the nineteenth century. A twelfth-century wooden predecessor of the present Ouse Bridge is said to have collapsed under the weight of the crowd who gathered to welcome Archbishop William to the city, and in the early fourteenth century the bridge on this site was supporting shops and houses. Overloading and pressure of broken ice floes brought about its collapse in 1565.

With new Tadcaster stone and bits of ruinous buildings in the city, this sixteenth-century bridge was rebuilt with a steeply-humped single arch (designed to discourage house builders) in the following year. A survivor of the collapse, the three-gabled council chamber, furnished with green upholstery, was a feature of the north side of the bridge. Near the council chamber was St. William's Chapel, a three-altar civic chapel with a needle spire and clock. Fragments of it are now in the Yorkshire Musuem.

Cast-iron Lendal Bridge, opened in 1863, replaced a ferry service dating back to the Middle Ages. John Leeman, last of the ferrymen, was compensated with a horse and cart and £15 in cash. A build-up of traffic in the 1870's called for another major bridge, downstream from Ouse Bridge, and after eight years of arguing and building, Skeldergate Bridge was opened in 1881. Of the city's half-dozen minor bridges, Blue Bridge and Foss Bridge are particularly attractive. The present Blue Bridge dates from 1929, but the first on this site was built in 1738 to connect St. George's Field with the fashionable, elm-shaded New Walk. It was painted blue, and the name has stuck. Today's bridge, the sixth on the site, was once flanked by two Russian guns taken from the Great Redan at Sebastopol during the Crimean War. Special stone platforms were built for them, and there they stayed until, about 1941, they were sold as scrap for the war effort.

The classical Foss Bridge, virtually unchanged since it was built in 1811-12 at the south-east end of Fossgate, is best seen from the river itself. Here again, houses intruded, and a plan made in the reign of Charles II shows properties on its south-west side.

There was a sort of "free bridge fever" on June 18th, 1829, 14th anniversary of Waterloo, when Ouse Bridge was freed from toll. Three men, their hats decorated with coloured ribbons, rode over the bridge on asses, and the arches reverberated to cannon shots from a ship moored underneath.

At the stroke of noon a carter, who had been waiting some time with a timber-laded rully on the south side, crossed over. He was followed by a brewer's dray and the Harrogate and Leeds mail-coaches (the Stockton and Darlington Railway was then only four years old). A band played the national anthem and the guards of each coach fired their blunderbusses. Tolls were collected on both Lendal and Skeldergate Bridges, the turreted toll-houses on Lendal Bridge now being used as shop premises.

Many of the old river photographs show the pleasure boat, River King, spreading its awning like a gunboat on the Zambezi, and it symbolises the affection York has always had for its ancient artery. Today tourists can take a trip downstream to the delights of Bishopthorpe (not only a riverside restaurant but a glimpse of the Archbishop's Palace too). In the last century much more ambitious trips were made. The first steamboat to be seen on the Ouse was the Waterloo, greeted by a crowd of sightseers on April 25, 1816. In time the passenger steamer, linked with train services, became as familiar as the long-distance coach of today. By 1836 the river steamer service was big business. In that year the York-London mail-coach still had six more years of life and the prospect of a 33-hour journey by water to the capital was quite acceptable. But by 1875 the passenger steamboat service had been swept away. In the early eighties of the last century a more restricted pleasure steamer service between York and its neighbouring riverside villages was begun.

The White Rose, the May Queen, the Waterlily and the Celia (a paddler) were all owned by John Hobson, a familiar figure on King's Staith. After his death, Edward Grace carried on the service with the River King.

The freezing of the Ouse is a widely-spaced phenomenon, probably occurring not more than half-a-dozen times in a century. In 1895 the river was frozen for at least a fortnight, a scene recalled in a letter written to the Yorkshire Evening Press in 1967. The writer's father, a railway clerk, skated to the office on the frozen river every day. Roast potatoes and chestnuts were sold on the ice.

One of the longest ice-bound spells fell in the winter of 1740 when booths were set up on the river and football matches on the frozen surface were common.

The huge broomhead which is to be seen hanging over Seale's Petergate brush shop in many old photographs was just one of the larger-than-life trade signs which decorated the city streets in the late eighteenth and nineteenth centuries. Though many of these long gone signs are preserved in the timeless settings of the York Castle Museum, forming part of the re-constructed streets there, two still survive in the cold light of the twentieth century. A snuff-taking Napoleon is a feature of a tobacconist's shop in Lendal, and a "cigar store" Indian of the kind made between 1790 and 1820 stands on a bracket over an antique shop in Low Petergate. A former tobacconist's, this shop has the added attraction of a small metal horse's head on the left-hand door lintel. A gas jet flared from its nostrils as an amenity for passing smokers who needed a light.

In the same field as the trade signs were the public house name-boards of the past—curious names like the Whale Fishery which stood at the corner of Haver Lane in the Hungate slums. It was given this name by the landlord, Christopher Bean, who had been a harpooner in the polar seas. The sign was a miniature carved whaling boat and a painting of a harpooner. The Old Sand Hill stood on the corner of Colliergate and St. Andrewgate, a site now occupied by a Drill Hall. It was a posting house with extensive stabling where, three days a week, a "pair-horse diligence" left for Malton and Scarborough. After Dick Turpin's execution in 1739 the corpse was taken to a back room of the Blue Boar in Castlegate to await burial in St. George's churchyard, and in 1814 a Roman tessellated pavement, found under the Jolly Bacchus near Micklegate Bar, was ruined by unchecked souvenir hunters.

Modern York, with a population of 107,000, has about 285 licensed premises, including public houses, restaurants and off-licence shops. But at the turn of the century there were at least 245 full-blown pubs distributed rather generously among a population of about 77,000. In a strictly alphabetical pub-crawl of the city in the nineties a reveller would have started at the Acorn in St. Martin's Lane and drunk his way through to the Yorkshireman in Coppergate. He might have been left with hazy memories of the Engine Driver's Rest in Mount Ephraim, the Garrick's Head in Low Petergate, the Glassblowers' Arms in the Cattle Market, the Ham And Firkin in Walmgate, the Boot And Slipper in Bedern, the Cannon in Lendal, the Lottery in Hull Road, the Sawdust Parlour in Swinegate, the Upholsterers' Arms in Trinity Lane and—perhaps oddest of all—the Barefoot in Micklegate.

One April evening in 1834—William IV's roustabout days—a fight broke out in a York public house. It was reported that "pitchers and glasses were demolished in the twinkling of an eye". On the face of it, there was nothing unusual in that, but when it was discovered who had been involved in the fight the story went round the city in a flash. That particular Thursday was the day set aside for the swearing-in of constables for the various city parishes. Two of them had been sworn in—perhaps unwisely—at a public house. The first thing the new constables did was to toast their success in quite a lot of brandy and water. One thing led to another, and when the question arose as to who should cope with the night work, they came to blows. That was when the pitchers and glasses hit the floor. The landlord had no option but to call another "keeper of the peace" to separate them. He settled the dispute and the quarrelsome constables filled their glasses again and drank to their renewed friendship. Little wonder there was a call for a unified and organised police force. It came into being in 1836 and the Corporation appointed a Watch Committee as required by the Municipal Corporations Act of the previous year. From a motley collection of assistants and parish constables, a force consisting of a superintendent, an inspector and ten constables was created. The city's first police station was that of the city commissioner's patrol in St. Andrewgate, but this was replaced by a better building in Silver Street in 1841.

It was in the July of that year that the force's effectiveness was questioned by the Grand Jury at the summer assizes. John Prest, jury foreman, said it was the general opinion that the police of the city were "not at all equal to its wants". There were only two men patrolling during the day. The judge, summing up in a manslaughter case, said that "under the very nose of the city police a cry of 'police' was raised which was heard by a policeman in the station house, and yet no assistance came, because it happened that only one person remained in the station." Apparently the other half of the city's day-time force was half a mile away at the time. We shall never know what stopped the station officer from answering the distress call.

Civic junketing in the early nineteenth century was on a generous level. When William Oldfield, wine merchant and postmaster, became Lord Mayor of York for the first time in 1825, he was given not only 32 hares, 87 partridges, 31 pheasants and three wild ducks, but a 14 lb. pike, two cucumbers, and a pot of shrimps. He had need of them all. Any citizen finding himself in possession of the Mansion House then would also find himself playing host on a colossal scale, and in the days of aldermanic trenchermen he would probably have reason to thank friends who sent him "food parcels" from their estates. Meals tended to last quite a while in those days. The King's Birthday Dinner, held on Saturday, April 23, 1825, started at 6 p.m. According to the Lord Mayor's notes, dessert was not reached until about nine, and it must be remembered that dessert alone could run to 15 or 20 items. Amenities at the Mansion House that night were very up-to-date. "Upon this occasion," the Lord Mayor recorded, "instead of the illumination by candles and transparencies, the Mansion House was illuminated by gas outside, by the letters G IV R, the size of the letters being three and a half feet. The expense of the illumination to me £NIL."

During a typical four-course Mansion House dinner of the period 69 items were on offer. Meats alone, in the first course, included fillets of veal, haunches and necks of venison, rounds of beef, saddles of mutton, game and pigeon pies, venison pasties, hams, tongues, roast geese and boiled turkeys, chickens and legs of lamb.

The lighting arrangements that so delighted William Oldfield had been part of the city scene for a little over a year.

There were crowds in the streets of York on the night of March 22, 1824. The Minster bells rang and most people were late to bed . . . gaslight had come into their lives. All three of the York newspapers—Courant, Chronicle and Gazette—were enthusiastic about the "new era of light in old Ebor" and contrasted the gas with the "dim and murky glare" of the oil lamps it had replaced. The Courant reported that "the large lamp in the Pavement had a very good effect. The fitting up of the light in the several shops is very splendid, and the large circular light over the door of Mr. Barber, at the Black Swan, was generally admired." The Chronicle had a look at the Theatre Royal which was "brilliantly illuminated, the saloon, lobbies and front of the boxes being hung with elegant chandeliers, lighted with gas." The Gazette found that "the streets for several hours presented the appearance of a fair, so eager were the inhabitants to witness the novel spectacle."

In the early days of gaslighting in York the lamps, about 300 in all, were not lit from dusk to dawn each night, nor throughout the whole year. They were divided into "eight month lamps" and "six month lamps", and to confuse things still further there were also "moonlight" lamps and "partial moonlight" lamps, which were not lighted on specified nights according to instructions issued from the Guildhall. It was not until 1849 that street lighting was continued throughout the year.

Gaslight at its best is to be seen in Half Moon Court, one of the world-famous "streets" in the York Castle Museum, where a Sugg's Lyttleton Lamp with six burners hangs over the Edwardian Fent and Drapery Stores. This type of lamp is often seen in photographs of the city streets at the turn of the century. It was popular with shopkeepers and some were adapted for use with an engraved advertising slide. The museum's specimen came from a fruit shop in Walmgate.

Gas-lamps of the wall bracket type still survive in a number of the intimate courts and alleys which go to make up the irreplaceable tangle of York's urban scene. Restored and gilded, they burn steadily on winter evenings, silent reminders of simpler days.

Skating on the River Ouse, February, 1895. (By courtesy of The Yorkshire Evening Press).

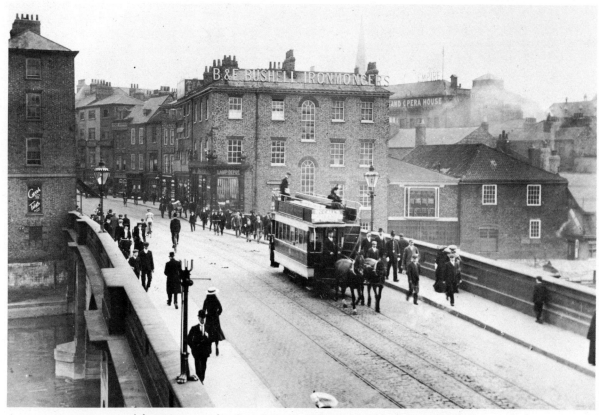

A horse-tram crossing Ouse Bridge in 1905 (By courtesy of The Yorkshire Evening Press).

A pair of Russian guns from the Crimea which once decorated Blue Bridge
near the junction of the Ouse and Foss rivers.

York from Lendal Bridge.

The River King coming upstream from Ouse Bridge to Lendal Bridge.
On the left, the Guildhall's river frontage and the tower of St. Martin-le-
Grand, Coney Street.

Decorated tram on the opening day of the electric service, January 20, 1910.
The battlemented building in the background is part of the Castle Wall,
demolished in the 1930's.

All Saints', Pavement. Carriers' carts and reapers stand at the east end.

Superb cast-iron detail is seen in this view of Platforms 5 and 6 at York Station.

— OLD ST MAURICE'S CHURCH — YORK 1868 —

Old St. Maurice's Church, on the corner of Monkgate and Lord Mayor's Walk in 1868. Demolished in the 1870's, it was succeeded by a much larger church, opened in 1878. This, in turn, was demolished in 1967.

A busy day in Blake Street as two traps pass, one driver bowler-hatted, the other wearing a top hat. A cyclist adjusts his clips outside a casement-windowed building, now gone. The public house in the background advertises John J. Hunt's Entire — short for "entire butt beer".

Opening of a trade exhibition in the Exhibition Buildings, c. 1911.

The "Swiss Cottage" style of temporary building erected in Bootham Park for the Industrial Exhibition of 1866.

Clifford's Tower, its mound tree-covered. On the right the gaol building and its surrounding wall, now demolished.

The two men with the delivery cart are outside Rowntree's original shop in Pavement, before rebuilding. On the left, Sir Thomas Herbert's House, its half-timbering hidden under a coat of stucco.

The York Herald Office, looking like a converted country town inn, was removed from Pavement when Piccadilly was extended in 1910. Just visible on the left, the south wall of St. Crux Church, demolished 1884-7. A parish room, containing some of the principal monuments, was built from the material on the same site.

Lofthouse's fruit and potato warehouse and Dawson's shaving rooms made way for W. P. Brown's present-day store on the corner of Davygate and St. Sampson's Square.

A sailing barge on the Ouse, downstream from Skeldergate Bridge.

Fossgate in 1900. A mass of advertising in this scene . . . paper bag warehouse, pictures framed, Hignett's smoking mixture, boots made to measure, Waverley pens—and a long barber's pole reaching out over the street. (By courtesy of the Yorkshire Architectural and York Archaeological Society).

St. Martin-le-Grand, Coney Street. Badly damaged by fire bombs in the Baedeker raid of April, 1942, part of the church was restored as a chapel of ease and a garden of rest. Re-hallowed in 1968, it retains the City's most famous clock, topped by a figure of a naval officer of the eighteenth century using a sextant.

Goodramgate c.1900 before the creation of Deangate. The opening half-way along on the left leads to College Street and St. William's College. The small building above now has its half-timbering revealed. The shops to the left were demolished when Deangate was cut through in 1903. (By courtesy of the Yorkshire Architectural and York Archaeological Society).

The partly-demolished St. Crux Church on the corner of Shambles and Pavement, 1884-7.

All Saints Church, North Street, offers the finest glass of any parish church in the city, set in windows which were dismantled and reassembled in the 1960's.

The old station was built in 1841, superseded in the 1870's and demolished in 1966. It was familiar to Charles Dickens, who visited the city not only to give his famous readings but to visit his brother and sister-in-law. (By courtesy of British Rail).

Low Petergate in the early 1880's. On the left may be seen the larger-than-life broomhead which advertised Seale's brush and mat warehouse. It is now in the York Castle Museum.

Laying tramlines in Blossom Street in the winter of 1910.

Run-down property in Walmgate in the 1930's.

The market in full swing in Parliament Street in 1889. The shoppers in the foreground are character studies, from the straw-hatted young man, thumbs in his waistcoat, to the policeman with his long sideburns and white gloves.

Nessgate in 1900 looking towards St. Michael's Church, Spurriergate. This block of property is now occupied by the Coach and Horses public house.

The corner of Low Ousegate and Nessgate, showing the predecessor of the
Coach and Horses, and the premises of John Rex, Assam tea dealer.

Micklegate before 1855, showing the gateway to the former Benedictine Priory, demolished during the building of Priory Street.

Water Lane, one of the medieval alleys which ran down to the river.

Boats moored at the site of the Lendal ferry, photographed by Roger
Fenton, the famous Crimean War photographer, in 1854.

The interior courtyard of St. William's College in the days when this
beautiful half-timbered building of the fifteenth century was covered in
stucco and split into tenements.

Narrow Little Blake Street (formerly Lop Lane) partly obscured the West Front of the Minster until it was expanded into the present Duncombe Place in the mid-nineteenth century.

The elaborate plasterwork front of the George Inn, Coney Street, as it was until demolished in the mid-nineteenth century.

The north side of High Ousegate in the early years of the century.

Premises in Pavement demolished to make way for the Piccadilly extension c. 1910.

The Shambles at the turn of the century.

The Plumbers' Arms, Skeldergate, demolished and rebuilt in the 1960's.